REMAINS TO BE SEEN

EXPLORING
THE INCAS

REMAINS TO BE SEEN

EXPLORING THE INCAS

JOHN MALAM

EVANS BROTHERS LIMITED

First published by
Evans Brothers Limited
2A Portman Mansions
Chiltern Street
London W1U 6NR

First published in this edition 2006
© text and illustrations in this edition 2006

Printed in Spain by GRAFO, S.A. - Bilbao

VISIT OUR WEBSITE
Evans
www.evansbooks.co.uk

ISBN 0 237 53153 4

13 - digit ISBN (from 1 January 2007)
978 0 237 53153 9

Acknowledgements

The author and publishers would like to thank the following
people for their valuable help and advice:

Dr George Bankes, Keeper of Ethnology, The Manchester
Museum, University of Manchester
Dr Frank Meddons, Assistant Curator, Archaeology and Local
History Centre of Passmore Edwards Museum
Margaret Sharman, author and archaeologist

Illustrations: Jeffery Burn
Maps: Jillie Luff, Bitmap Graphics

Editor: Jean Coppendale
Design: Neil Sayer
Production: Jenny Mulvanny

For permission to reproduce copyright material the author and
publishers gratefully acknowledge the following:

Cover photograph: Machu Picchu, the lost city of the Incas. Roger
Coggan, Bruce Coleman Limited

Title page: M. Timothy O'Keefe, Bruce Coleman Limited

page 7 (top right) Tony Morrison, South American Pictures, (top
left) Tony Morrison, South American Pictures, (bottom left)
Werner Forman Archive/Dallas Museum of Fine Art, (middle
right) Werner Forman Archive/Dallas Museum of Fine Art page 8
Tony Morrison, South American Pictures page 9 Mireille Vautier,
E.T. Archive page 10 (top) Heinz Plenge, Robert Harding Picture
Library, (bottom) Robert Harding Picture Library page 11 (top)
Heinz Plenge, Robert Harding Picture Library, (middle) Mireille
Vautier, E.T. Archive, (bottom) Heinz Plenge, Robert Harding
Picture Library page 12 E.T. Archive page 14 H.R. Dorig, The
Hutchison Library page 15 E.T. Archive page 16 (top) Derrick
Furlong, Robert Harding Picture Library, (bottom) E.T. Archive
page 17 E.T. Archive page 18 Mireille Vautier, E.T. Archive

page 19 (top) Andre Bartschi, Bruce Coleman Limited, (bottom)
Tony Morrison, South American Pictures page 20 (top) E.T. Archive,
(bottom) K. Rodgers, The Hutchison Library, (inset) H.R. Dorig, The
Hutchison Library page 21 (top) Robert Harding Picture Library,
(bottom left and right) H.R. Dorig, The Hutchison Library page 22
(top) Michael Holford, (middle) Tony Morrison, South American
Pictures page 23 (top) Werner Forman Archive/The British Museum,
(bottom left) Mireille Vautier, E.T. Archive, (bottom right) H.R.
Dorig, The Hutchison Library pages 24/25 H.R. Dorig, The
Hutchison Library page 25 (right) Robert Harding Picture Library,
(left) Mireille Vautier, E.T. Archive page 26 Mireille Vautier, E.T.
Archive page 27 (top) Marion Morrison, South American Pictures,
(bottom left) Udo Hirsch, Bruce Coleman Limited, (bottom right) M.
Timothy O'Keffe, Bruce Coleman Limited page 28 H.R. Dorig, The
Hutchison Library page 29 (top) Mark Cole, (middle) Carlos Reyes,
Andes Press Agency, (bottom) H.R. Dorig, The Hutchison Library
page 30 (top) Carlos Reyes, Andes Press Agency, (bottom) H.R.
Dorig, The Hutchison Library page 31 (top) Edward Parker, South
American Pictures, (bottom left) E.T. Archive, (bottom right) Carlos
Reyes, Andes Press Agency page 32 H.R. Dorig, The Hutchison
Library, page 33 Walter Rawlings, Robert Harding Picture Library
page 34 Robert Harding Picture Library/National Museum of
Archaeology, Lima page 35 Tony Morrison, South American
Pictures page 36 (left) M. Timothy O'Keefe, Bruce Coleman Limited,
(right) Mireille Vauteir, E.T. Archive page 37 Heniz Plenge, Robert
Harding Picture Library page 38 (top) H.R. Dorig, The Hutchison
Library, (bottom) Robert Harding Picture Library page 39 (top) H.R.
Dorig, The Hutchison Library, (bottom) Kerstin Rodgers, The
Hutchison Library page 40 Micheal Holford page 41 (left) H.R.
Dorig, The Hutchison Library, (middle) E.T. Archive, (right) Mary
Evans Picture Library page 42 (bottom) E.T. Archive pages 42/43
Norman Owen Tomalin, Bruce Coleman Limited page 43 (bottom
left) M.P.L. Fogden, Bruce Coleman Limited, (bottom right) Giorgio
Gualco, Bruce Coleman Limited page 44 (top) Heinz Plenge, Robert
Harding Picture Library, (bottom) Heinz Plenge, Robert Harding
Picture Library page 45 (top) Mireille Vautier, E.T. Archive,
(bottom) T. McDonald, Panos Pictures.

Contents

TIMELINE OF THE INCAS

and the rest of the world

WORLD HISTORY	YEAR	INCA HISTORY
c.1000 Vikings sail to Vinland (Newfoundland) 1066 Norman conquest of England 1090s First Crusade to the Holy Land	AD1000	
1187 Jerusalem is recaptured from the Crusaders	AD1100	
1200s Aztecs established an empire in Mexico 1200s Rise of the Mongol empire in Europe and Asia 1271–95 Marco Polo travels to China	AD1200	1200 Manco Capac – the legendary first Inca emperor and founder of the city of Cuzco
1300s Great Zimbabwe city built in Africa 1337–1453 Hundred Years War between England and France 1347–53 Black Death plague in Europe	AD1300	
1455–85 Wars of the Roses in England 1492 Christopher Columbus sails to the 'New World' 1497 John Cabot sails to Newfoundland	AD1400	1438–71 Reign of Pachacuti Inca Yupanqui who greatly expanded the Inca empire

1500s First slaves taken to the Americas
        from Africa
 	
1521   Spaniards conquer Aztec empire
 	
1588   Spanish Armada defeated by English
        fleet
	AD1500	1525–32 Reign of Huascar, half-
		brother of Atahuallpa
		1532–33 Reign of Atahuallpa, the
		thirteenth and the last Inca
		emperor
		1532 Spaniards land at Tumbes, led
		by Francisco Pizarro
		1532 Atahuallpa taken prisoner by
		Pizarro at Cajamarca
		1533 Atahuallpa executed
		1570s Incas leave the city of Machu
		Picchu
		Late 1500s Guamán Poma writes a
		history of the Incas entitled
		'The First New Chronicle and
		Good Government',
		sometimes called 'Letter to a
		King'

1607 First English colonists settle in America 1620 English Puritans sail to America on Mayflower 1642–46 English Civil War 1664 New York named by British settlers	AD1600	1600 Guamán Poma's 'Letter to a King' is sent to King Philip III of Spain

Objects from the time of the Incas

An Inca sun god mask made of gold. ▶

▼ Inca keru, or wooden drinking vessel, shaped to look like the head of a jaguar.

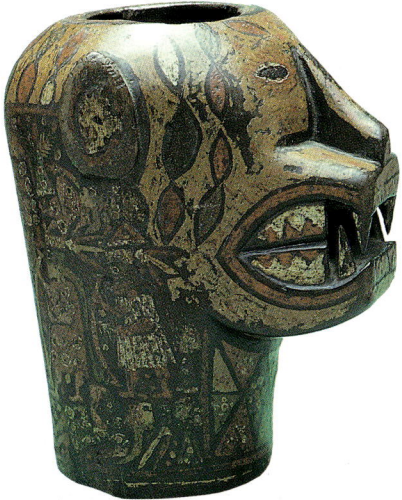

A very ornate tunic covered in small squares of gold. It would have belonged to an Inca noble. Imagine how it must have shone in the sun.

A small 'breastplate' woven from feathers and showing the figure of a god.

WHO WERE THE INCAS?

Introduction to the Incas

The Incas lived in South America, about 500 years ago. They ruled over a large and powerful empire which developed very quickly, but only lasted for about 100 years, between AD 1438 and 1533. The Inca homeland was in the present-day country of Peru. As their empire grew, it stretched along the western edge of South America, from Ecuador in the north to Chile in the south – a distance of about 4,000 kilometres. Within this great area the landscape was enormously varied. Hot, sandy deserts near the coast gave way to plains of fertile pasture inland, semi-tropical forests, deep valleys, and the high snow-capped mountains of the Andes.

It is estimated that between seven and ten million people lived within the Inca empire. They belonged to more than 100 different groups of people, each of which spoke their own local language. To control their vast empire, the Incas used an official language called Quechua (see page 19) and built a network of roads (see page 28), all of which were connected to their capital at Cuzco.

Today, the Pacific coast of Peru is one of the world's driest deserts. In the time of the Incas it was irrigated with fresh water and fields of vegetables were grown there.

The Inca Empire

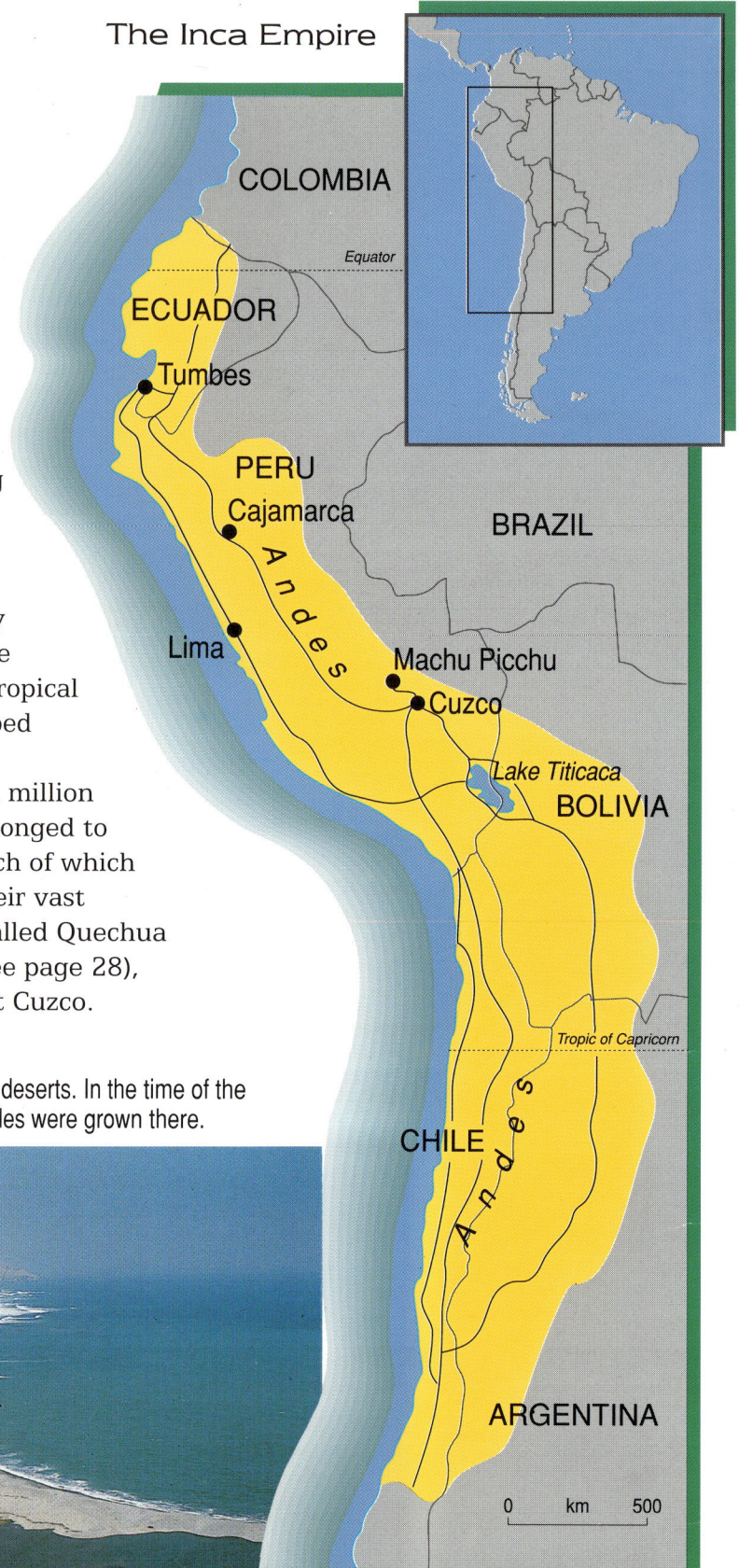

	Extent of the Inca Empire
	Inca road network
	Present day boundary
PERU	Present day country name

The Urubamba Valley clearly shows the varied landscape of Peru. The fertile valley floor is a patchwork of small fields beyond which rise the snow-capped Andes mountains. The name Andes comes from 'Antis' – an Inca word given by them to groups of people who lived in the rainforests. Today, 60 per cent of Peru is still rainforest, most of which is protected by law from damage.

The Incas were the last of the great ancient civilizations of South America. With the arrival of European invaders in the 1500s, their empire collapsed. Today, we can learn about the Incas from a number of sources. These include archaeological excavations which uncover remains of actual Inca settlements and objects, eyewitness reports written by the first Europeans who met them, and accounts by native writers such as the famous 'letter' written by Guamán Poma (see opposite). By studying all this evidence, we are able to find out about the lost world of the Incas.

Lake Titicaca is the world's highest navigable lake at 3,800 metres above sea level. To the Incas it was a sacred place and to the Spaniards it was where a great treasure of gold was hidden. In the 1970s the French explorer Jacques Cousteau used mini submarines to explore the lake – but he found no gold.

Fact File

The 'letter' of Guamán Poma

Guamán Poma, whose name means 'falcon puma', was not an Inca, but a chieftain from a small Peruvian tribe that was conquered by the Incas. He lived at the time of the Inca empire and witnessed the arrival of the Spaniards (see page 40). He realized the world of the Incas was going to change for ever and decided to write to King Philip III of Spain, describing the Incas' history and lifestyle and showing how everything was changing under Spanish rule. He learned how to write in Spanish, and for 50 years he recorded every aspect of Inca life, in words and pictures. He called his life's work 'Letter to a King' and when he was nearly 90 years old (in the early 1600s), he sent his great story to Spain. But King Philip may never have seen it. Instead, the Danish Ambassador to Spain bought Guamán Poma's 'letter' and took it to Copenhagen – which is where it is today. In 1908 a German scholar discovered the 'letter' in the Royal Library of Copenhagen and much of what we know today about the Incas comes from Guamán Poma's remarkable work of 1200 pages and 400 drawings.

In Guamán Poma's 'Letter to a King' he drew a picture of himself presenting his story of Inca life to King Philip III of Spain. Note how he imagined himself, dressed in the fine clothes of a Spanish noble. We know that Guamán Poma never went to Spain and it is unlikely that the king ever saw the letter that was addressed to him.

Peru before the Incas

Peru has a long history that stretches back for thousands of years before the time of the Incas. Many different groups of people have lived there, each with its own distinctive identity.

One of Peru's earliest civilizations grew up along the country's northern coast from about AD 100 to 600. The people of this civilization were called the Moche. They lived in steep-sided river valleys. The Moche people grew maize, beans, peppers, avocados and squash (a kind of fruit). They ate llamas, guinea-pigs and fish.

One of the largest Moche towns was at Pampa Grand, in the Lambayeque Valley. As many as 10,000 people might have lived there.

The Moche built gigantic pyramids and platforms out of sun-dried mud-brick. The pyramid called Huaca del Sol (the Pyramid of the Sun) stands 45 metres high and was built from over one hundred million mud-bricks! Today, it is still one of the largest man-made buildings in South America and is 1,500 years old.

In 1987, a fabulous discovery was made at Sipán. The graves of several important people were found, buried deep inside a mud-brick platform. The most important grave was that of a Moche king who had died aged about 30. His body was covered from head to toe with objects of gold, silver and copper. He wore a mask of gold over his face and copper sandals on his feet. He could not have walked in them – he probably wore them as a sign to show he was a king. Around the coffin of the Moche king were the bodies of several other men and women. Some had had one or both of their feet removed, as if to stop them from ever leaving the side of their royal master. Even the king's dog was buried in the mass grave!

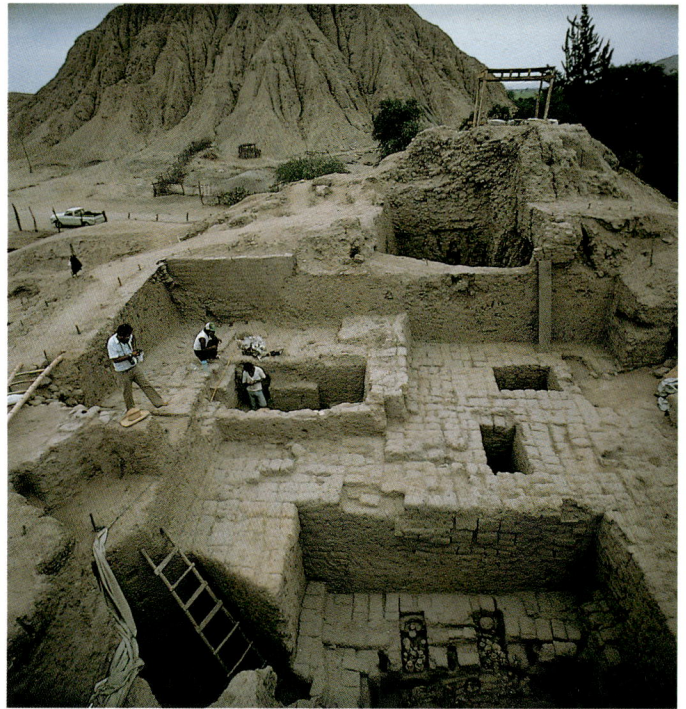

In the background is the 1,700-year-old mud-brick pyramid at Sipán, worn by the weather into a strange shape. In front of it is a platform of mud-brick where the Moche buried their king in the square pit in the foreground, seen here during its excavation in 1987.

This strange gold object is a Moche hand rattle. Its sound came from small copper balls placed inside the 10 gold spheres around its edge. The figure in the centre is the so-called 'decapitator god' who holds a knife in his left hand and a human head in his right. The object came from the tomb of the Moche king.

The burial of the Moche king at Sipán, covered by the archaeologists' string grid which was used to help them record the remains. The king was buried inside a wooden coffin and wore the fine clothes of a royal leader. He was covered in objects of gold, silver and copper. On his chest were 11 fan-shaped breastplates made from copper beads and shells and his body lay on top of a large gold headdress, part of which can be seen to the left of the skeleton. Despite the great amount of information which came from the tomb the identity of the king is still a mystery. Archaeologists have named him the 'Lord of Sipán'.

Copper mask from the tomb of the Moche king. It is covered by a thin skin of gold and has fangs of shell. It may represent a jaguar.

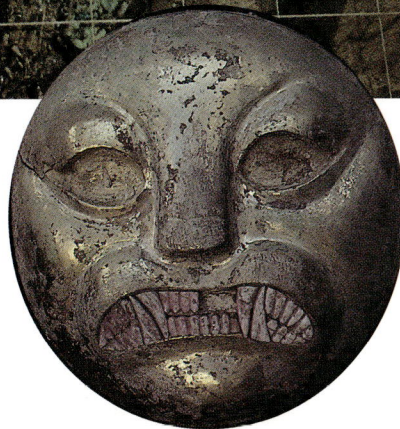

The great hole made by tomb robbers before archaeologists heard about the site at Sipán.

Fact File

Tomb robbers at Sipán

Driven by greed, local people had broken into the mud-brick mound in search of gold and valuables. Before archaeologists reached Sipán, many precious objects had been taken from the mound and illegally exported out of Peru. The government of Peru acted quickly and a proper excavation began. It was during this excavation that archaeologists found the grave of the Moche king – undisturbed after 1,700 years. The quick-fingered tomb robbers had missed the greatest treasure of them all! Even though the robbers had dug a massive hole into the mound, they stopped their digging when they were about two metres away from the king's burial place. Had they found it, then the treasures seen on this page would have been stolen and sold, and we would know nothing about them.

THE EMPIRE OF THE INCAS

How the empire began

'Who were the Incas?' and 'Where did they come from? These are important questions, but neither is very easy to answer.

The west coast of South America had been the homeland of many different peoples before the Inca civilization. Each group had its own way of life, its own language and its own land – Peru was really a land divided into many small 'states'.

The Incas belonged to one of these states and their small population was made up of many related families. Their capital was at Cuzco (see page 24). It was from Cuzco that the empire of the Incas began to spread beyond their traditional homeland. Archaeologists believe that the empire really began in the reign of the ninth Inca emperor, Pachacuti Inca Yupanqui. In a little less than 100 years, between about 1438 and 1533, the Incas conquered the land of neighbouring tribes and brought it under their control. At the height of their power, the Incas ruled an empire which had a population of between seven and ten million people.

Fact File

The word 'Inca'

The word 'Inca' can be used in several different ways. At first, it was used to refer to the original families who all spoke the same Inca language and who lived in and around Cuzco. When the Spaniards arrived in the early 16th century they used the word 'Inca' to refer to all the people that lived in the Inca empire, regardless of the language they actually spoke. The Incas themselves would never have done this, since they regarded the conquered people in their empire as 'foreigners', not real Incas. The Spaniards also used the word to refer to the leader of the Incas, whom they simply called 'The Inca', meaning the chief of the Incas.

The Incas were curious about their origins, and they told stories to explain where they believed they came from. According to an Inca legend, the first Inca family (four brothers and four sisters) emerged from a cave about 30 kilometres south-east of Cuzco. They carried with them a rod of gold which had been given to them by their father, Inti, the the sun god. They were to walk until they found a place where the rod would disappear into the ground. This place would then become their home. When they arrived at Cuzco the rod sank into the ground, and so it was here that they settled. The legend says that Manco Capac and his sister, Mama Huaco, were from the first family and they were the ancestors of all the Inca people.

Portrait of the emperor Pachacuti, painted many years after his death. It is not known if he looked like this in real life.

The Inca legend of Manco Capac and his sister, Mama Huaco, as they tested the soil with a magic rod of gold. Where the soil was good enough to grow crops, it would sink into the ground. The rod went into the soil at Cuzco and the Inca capital was founded there.

Conquests of the Incas

At first, the Inca royal family and their followers were content to live in villages in the Cuzco valley. All around them lived different, rival peoples. From time to time the Incas would go to war against these groups, but they usually preferred them to join their empire voluntarily. Only when it became clear that a group was unwilling to co-operate would the Incas use violence. The Incas were not people to make enemies of.

After about 200 years of quarrelling with people from nearby villages who were not Incas, an Inca ruler in the 1400s (possibly Pachacuti) decided to get tough. With an army of soldiers drawn from conquered groups and led by Incas, Pachacuti marched further and further afield, defeating rival kingdoms and adding their land to the growing Inca empire.

Inca officials lived in and governed the captured land. They raised taxes by putting the conquered people to work to produce goods which were then either sent back to Cuzco or placed in storehouses elsewhere in the empire. The emperors who came after Pachacuti added more land to the empire until it reached its maximum extent in the 1530s, under the last Inca emperor, Atahuallpa.

Organizing the army was essential if the Incas wished to control their empire successfully. Roads were built throughout the land, bridges were constructed over ravines, and supply depots were established at fixed points. All this enabled the army to move quickly and comfortably in the knowledge that food and extra weapons were always nearby in the supply bases.

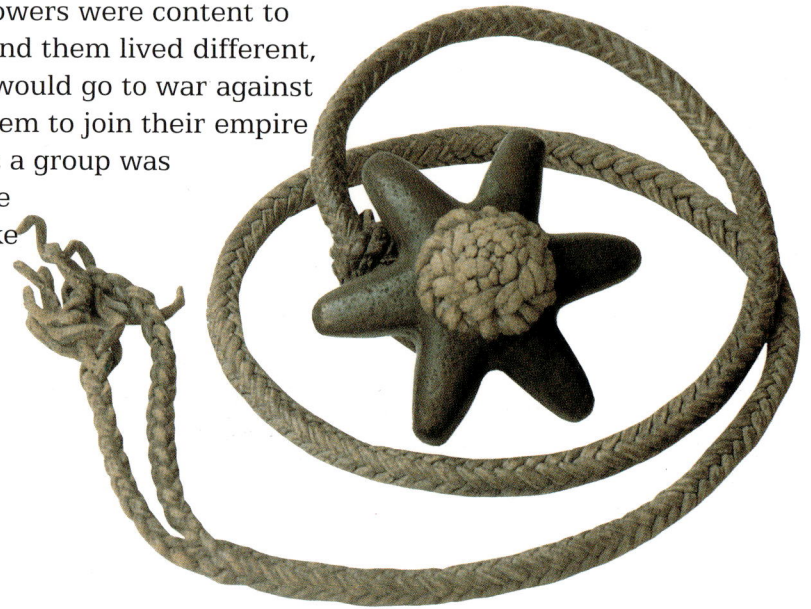

A star-shaped bronze weapon, used like a flail, or whip, at close quarters.

A drawing by Guamán Poma of an Inca soldier removing the eyes of a defeated enemy. His hands are tied behind his back and a guard holds the rope.

Fact File

Defeated enemies

The Incas had a very original way of treating their defeated enemies. To prevent rebellions from newly conquered people, a whole group was sometimes moved to another part of the empire. They were forbidden from ever returning home. People who had already been overcome and who had become peaceful farmers were given the land of the defeated tribe. The Incas called this practice 'mitima' and it broke the spirit of the defeated tribe so much that they lost the will to fight. In this way the Incas managed to keep their huge empire together.

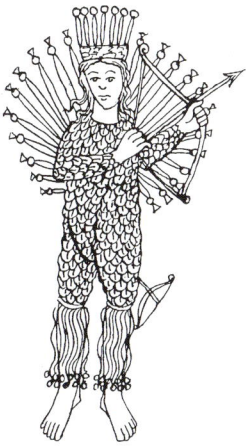

A drawing by Guamán Poma of a bowman dressed in a coat of feathers. He belonged to one of the forest tribes conquered by the Incas.

An Inca warrior carrying a spear painted on the side of a wooden vase. His body is protected with a kind of armour made from padded cotton and wickerwork.

Inca emperors and nobles

At the head of the Inca empire was the emperor. His official title was Sapa Inca which meant the 'unique' or 'only' Inca. The people in the empire thought of their emperor as a living god, put on Earth by Inti, the sun god, from whom he was descended.

The emperor was lord of all. He lived in a royal place at Cuzco where he was hidden from public gaze behind a wall. People could not look at the emperor's face except on very special occasions. Those that went to see him approached barefoot. All the food he left after meals and the clothes he threw out were

The earlobes of this man from the rainforests of the Amazon have been pierced and stretched into large loops inside which flat stones are worn for decoration. Inca nobles did the same with their ears and ear-plugs made of gold and feathers were worn in the loops.

An 18th century painting of an Inca emperor wearing his fine clothes and jewellery. On his chest is a gold pendant in the shape of the sun.

A drawing by Guamán Poma of an emperor's wife being attended by her maids. One combs and the other washes the coya's hair.

LAONZENACOIA
RAVAOCLLO

carefully saved. Once a year they were burned at a great ceremony.

The emperor was allowed to have many wives, but the wife he called his 'coya' was the most important queen. She was also thought to be a descendent of the sun and was the emperor's own sister.

When the emperor died, some of his wives and servants were executed (by strangling) so that they could follow him into the next world. His body was preserved and on important occasions it was brought into the main square at Cuzco where it was displayed with the dried bodies of older emperors. His palace became his tomb and shrine.

The emperor was surrounded by many high-ranking Inca nobles. They held important positions in his government and it was they who actually organized the empire. The nobles wore special clothes made from precious wool or feathers and only they could wear gold and silver jewellery. These were the signs of their noble class. They were well educated and were taught in Inca schools where people who were not Incas or nobles could not go.

Fact File

Inca emperors

It was because of the power of the royal family that the Incas were able to build their vast empire and control so many other tribes in South America. Here are the names of the 13 Inca emperors and the dates when they reigned. They were all thought to be descended from the legendary first Inca, Manco Capac (see page 12).

1. *Manco Capac (about AD 1200)*
2. *Sinchi Roca (about 1230)*
3. *Lloque Yupanqui (about 1260)*
4. *Mayta Capac (about 1290)*
5. *Capac Yupanqui (about 1320)*
6. *Inca Roca (about 1350)*
7. *Yahuar Huacac (about 1380)*
8. *Viracocha Inca (about 1410)*
9. *Pachacuti Inca Yupanqui (1438–1471)*
10. *Topa Inca Yupanqui (1471–1493)*
11. *Huayna Capac (1493–1525)*
12. *Huascar (1525–1532)*
13. *Atahuallpa (1532–1533)*

Today, we are used to our kings and queens usually inheriting their titles directly from one of their parents. But in Peru, it was the custom for the son of the emperor's sister to inherit the title. This was why an Inca emperor married his own sister, in order to guarantee that the title should still be handed down to his own son! (If he didn't marry this way then the title would be passed on to the emperor's nephew.)

This painting was made by a Spanish artist in an attempt to record the complete dynasty of Inca emperors. The two standing figures represent Manco Capac and his sister Mama Huaco.

THE WORLD OF THE INCAS

Organization of everyday life

For such a large empire to run smoothly it had to be well organized. Most of this was carried out by Inca nobles on behalf of the emperor. The empire was divided into four provinces. These were, in turn, divided into smaller units containing a number of households.

The whole of the population was divided into age groups and given duties to perform, such as building roads or farming the land. Even children had work to do, collecting wild plants in the woods for the emperor. Older children tended flocks of llamas, while elderly people watched over them. The Incas paid taxes through their labour – by building roads and farming the land, for example.

Most Incas lived in small villages, although some lived in large towns such as the capital Cuzco. Many new towns and

SESTA CALLE
CORO·TASQVE

A drawing by Guamán Poma of a 12-year-old girl tending llamas, collecting firewood and spinning wool – three tasks which were meant to be of help to her parents.

This is how an Inca house looked. Its walls were made of carefully cut stone and its roof was of wooden poles covered with thatched reeds. There could be either one or two rooms inside.

A group of people who live in a village in Peru today.

Fact File

Language and literature

The official language of the Incas was called 'Quechua', which was spoken in over 600 different dialects. 'Quechua' is still spoken in parts of Peru today. Unfortunately for us, the Incas did not know how to write, so we have no accounts written by the Incas about themselves – but we do have some written by Spanish explorers who visited the Inca empire when it was at its height in the 1500s. They tell us that the Incas loved stories in the form of long poems. Specially trained poets learned how to remember sagas about the history of the Incas, and at certain times they would recount them in the form of sung or spoken ballads. The sagas were passed on by word of mouth from one generation to the next.

villages were built thoughout the empire, usually in areas conquered by the Inca army. Inca people were moved into the new towns and officials were there to organize them. In this way the growing empire took on more and more of the Inca ways of life, making it harder for the conquered groups to carry on their old ways.

The Incas had a very unusual and confusing way of describing members of their immediate family. A mother would sometimes use the same name for both boys and girls, whereas the father would use different names to tell them apart! But when the father called a boy his 'son', he might have been referring to other relatives such as nephews! The terms brother and sister were often used to describe cousins, and father and mother might have been used instead of uncle or aunt. Names such as Happy, Tobacco or Condor were popular for boys, and Star, Gold or Egg for girls.

An open-air market in Peru today, selling a variety of products including brightly-coloured textiles.

Farming the land

Did you know that potatoes were first grown in Peru? Can you imagine what your meals would be like without potatoes? No crisps or French fries! We have a lot to thank the Incas for!

The Incas lived mainly by farming. Those that lived in the highlands grew potatoes and raised llamas and alpacas, while those that lived in the valleys grew maize and cotton. It is said that the Incas grew many different kinds of potato, far more than are grown today. Some kinds were specially developed to grow high up in the thin mountain soil.

The Incas farmed the slopes of steep mountains by building terraces along their sides. The terraces were held up by stone walls and rose from the floors of valleys to the tops of the highest peaks. Terraces followed the shape of the land and from a distance the mountains looked as if they had gigantic steps carved into them. Fertile soil was spread along the terraces and water was brought to them by specially made irrigation channels. Some channels flowed for hundreds of kilometres and brought fresh water from melting snow and ice in the high mountains. The terrace soil was kept fertile by spreading fertilizer on it. Animal

On this plate are four corn cobs – preserved since the time of the Incas.

Farmland of the Incas in the Urubamba Valley, one of Peru's most fertile areas. The terraces on the side of this mountain were made by Inca farmers with soil brought from the fertile river valley below. Every piece of land that could be farmed was farmed and many of these thin, ribbon-like fields are still being farmed today. *Inset:* A Peruvian farmer using a digging stick which is remarkably similar to ones used by his Inca ancestors, 500 years ago.

and human manure was used, but bird droppings called 'guano' was thought to be the best. Farmers who lived along the Pacific coast collected the 'guano' from offshore islands. It made the soil fertile so that they could grow food all year round.

Apart from potatoes, Inca farmers grew maize, peppers, peanuts, avocados, cotton and several kinds of beans. A rare orchid flower was grown for a medicine, as was coca, a plant whose leaves were chewed to help fight hunger, thirst and pain.

This is an alpaca, which is smaller than a llama. The Incas kept alpacas for the high-quality wool they gave.

Llamas were used as beasts of burden to carry goods throughout the empire, and they are still used this way by Peruvians today. Llamas were sacrificed at certain religious ceremonies in the Inca year.

Fact File

Counting

The Incas did not know how to write, but they developed a sophisticated counting and record-keeping system based on tying knots in string. The number of llamas owned by a farmer, the amount of maize he grew, or the number of people in a village could be recorded on a piece of knotted string called a 'quipu'. This was a long piece of strong cord tied to which were strings divided into groups. The strings were of different colours, representing different objects or people. Knots tied in the strings stood for numbers from single units up to 100,000 – the largest number that could be used. The 'quipu' also served as a memory aid in the telling of myths and sagas.

A drawing by Guamán Poma of a man holding a 'quipu'. To the Incas he was known as a 'quipucamayoc' which meant 'keeper of the quipus'. These men were only able to read those quipus which had been explained to them. The information which the quipus held could be passed down through generations of quipu keepers.

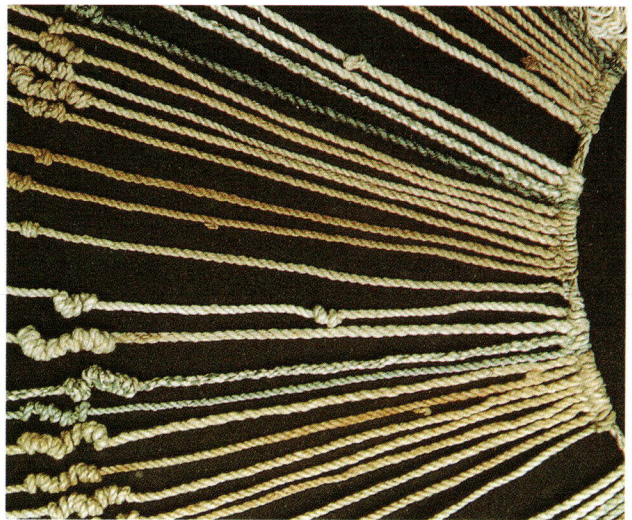

An example of a 'quipu'. The strings are different colours and contain many knots of information which the Incas could read – but we cannot.

Crafts of the Incas

The Incas were skilled crafts-people – and apart from textiles and pottery they excelled in working with gold, silver and bronze.

Goldwork

Gold was highly prized in Peru for hundreds of years before the coming of the Incas. They searched the length and breadth of their empire to find gold, which they dug from the ground and sifted from river beds. Gold was thought to be the tear drops of the sun. It was beaten into thin sheets and then fashioned into ornaments such as delicate pieces of jewellery and objects for use in religious ceremonies. Inca goldsmiths became some of the most skilful and highly regarded of all ancient metalworkers. When the Spaniards arrived they were tempted by the gold and the Incas' rich empire was soon plundered (see page 40), and many wonderful objects were taken back to Spain and melted down.

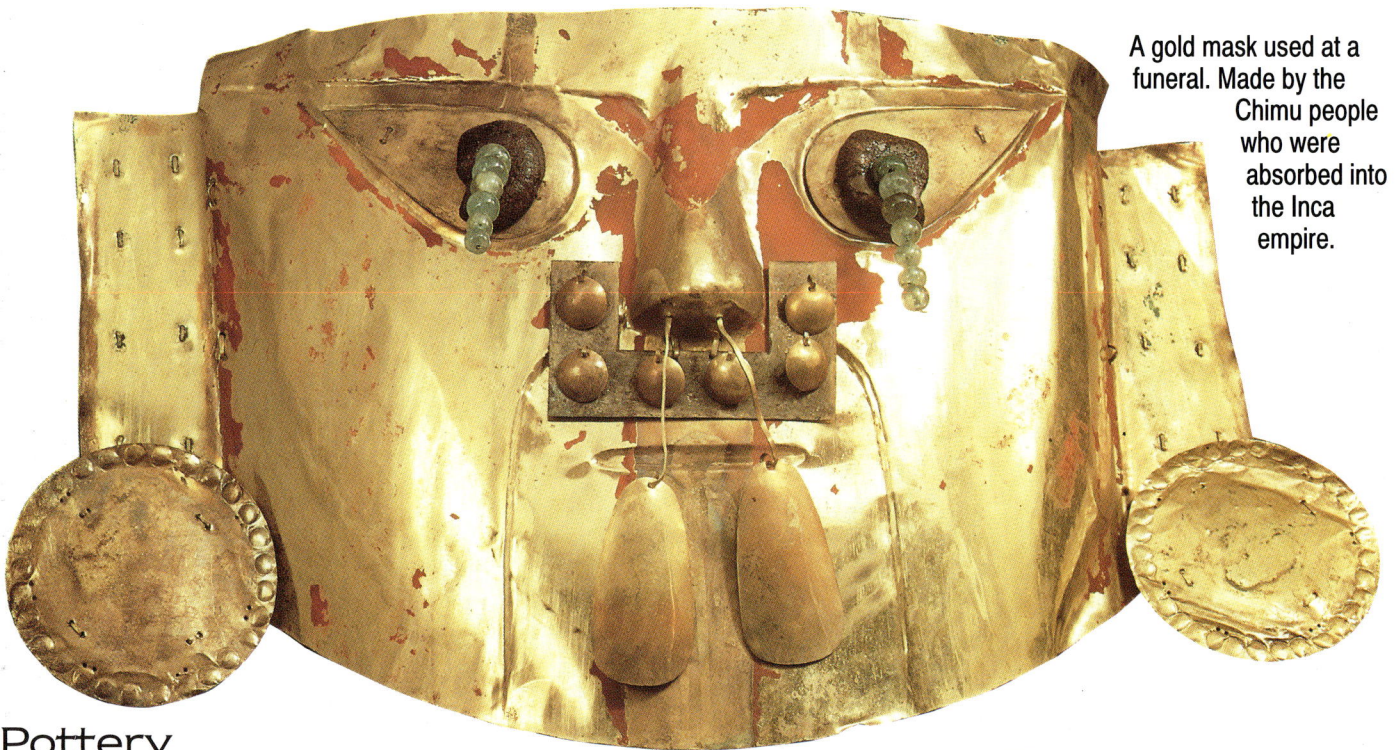

A gold mask used at a funeral. Made by the Chimu people who were absorbed into the Inca empire.

Pottery

It's hard to believe that the Incas did not know how to make pottery on a revolving potter's wheel. All their wonderful pots, large and small, plain and fantastically shaped, were slowly built up from coils of clay while others were made in moulds. The pots were dried in the sun and then their surfaces were smoothed over, making them shiny. Painted decorations were also applied at this time. Then they were baked in an oven to make them hard and waterproof.

A large Inca pot called an 'aryballus'. It was carried by a rope which passed through its two loop handles.

Textiles

Few examples of Inca textiles have been found. But pieces that have been discovered, in the dry coastal area, show that the Incas were expert weavers. Coarse wool from llamas, fine wool from

alpacas, together with cotton, was spun into yarns. The finest and most valuable wool came from the vicuña, a relative of the llama. Dyes were made from plant leaves, stems, roots, berries, minerals and even insects. They were all used to stain the yarns which women then wove into cloth. If the material was for the Inca royal family, yarns with an amazing range of bright colours were used and further decorated with intricate patterns. Feathers and thin pieces of gold and silver were sewn on to special pieces of cloth to give them even more decoration. Patterns were also made from small shells sewn on to cloth.

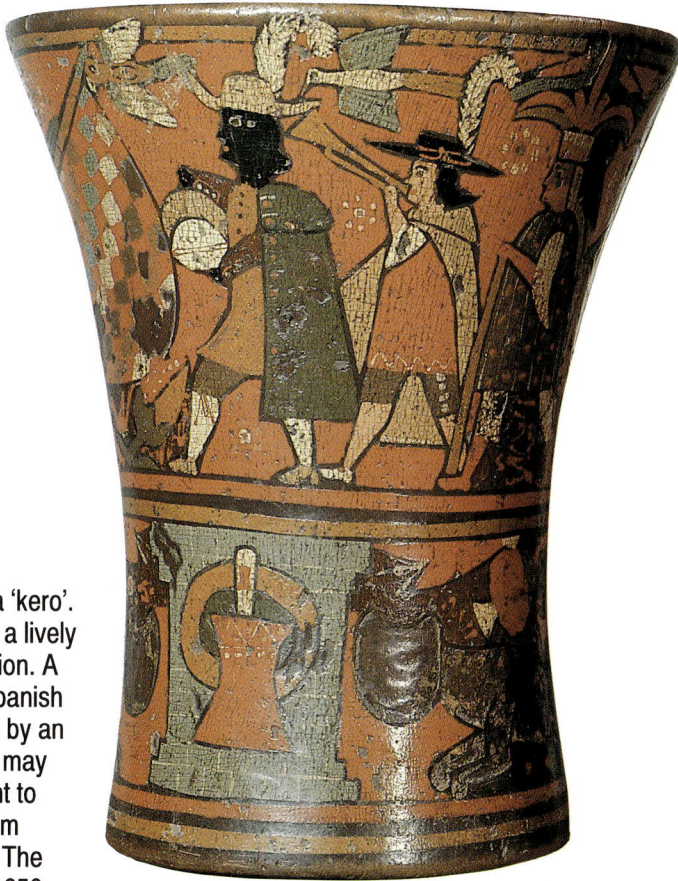

A wooden beaker called a 'kero'. Its surface is painted with a lively scene showing a procession. A black drummer leads a Spanish trumpeter who is followed by an Inca noble. The drummer may have been a slave brought to Peru by the Spaniards from Africa or the West Indies. The beaker was made about 1650.

An Inca tunic decorated with geometric patterns. The opening for the wearer's head can just be seen in the centre at the top.

Making cloth in a village in Peru today. This woman is weaving on a loom known as a backstrap loom. It is tied to a tree and she keeps it in tension by leaning backwards while working. Inca weavers would have looked similar to this weaver.

Cuzco – capital of the Incas

Cuzco was the capital city of the Incas. Its name means 'navel' in the Quechua (Inca) language, as it was built at the point where the empire's four provinces met. It was the very centre of the Inca world.

According to an Inca legend, Cuzco was founded by Manco Capac (see page 12). But archaeologists believe the city really began during the reign of the emperor Pachacuti, about 550 years ago. He kept a large workforce that built the city within his own lifetime. At its height, as many as 300,000 people are thought to have lived in Cuzco and its surrounding areas. They came from all parts of the Inca empire.

The city's buildings were made of stone with thatched roofs. The huge blocks of stone fitted together so closely that not even the blade of a knife could slip between them. Some temples in the religious centre of Cuzco were built from a dark red stone which stood out well from the city's otherwise grey buildings. Inside the main temples were priceless tapestries and vast amounts of gold and silver. Important ceremonies took place in the temples which were home to high-ranking priests.

Cuzco itself was not fortified but a massive fortress was built on a nearby hill to defend the city from attack. The fortress was called Sacsahuaman. Its strong stone walls still stand 16 metres high today, but 550 years ago they stood taller. In times of trouble the

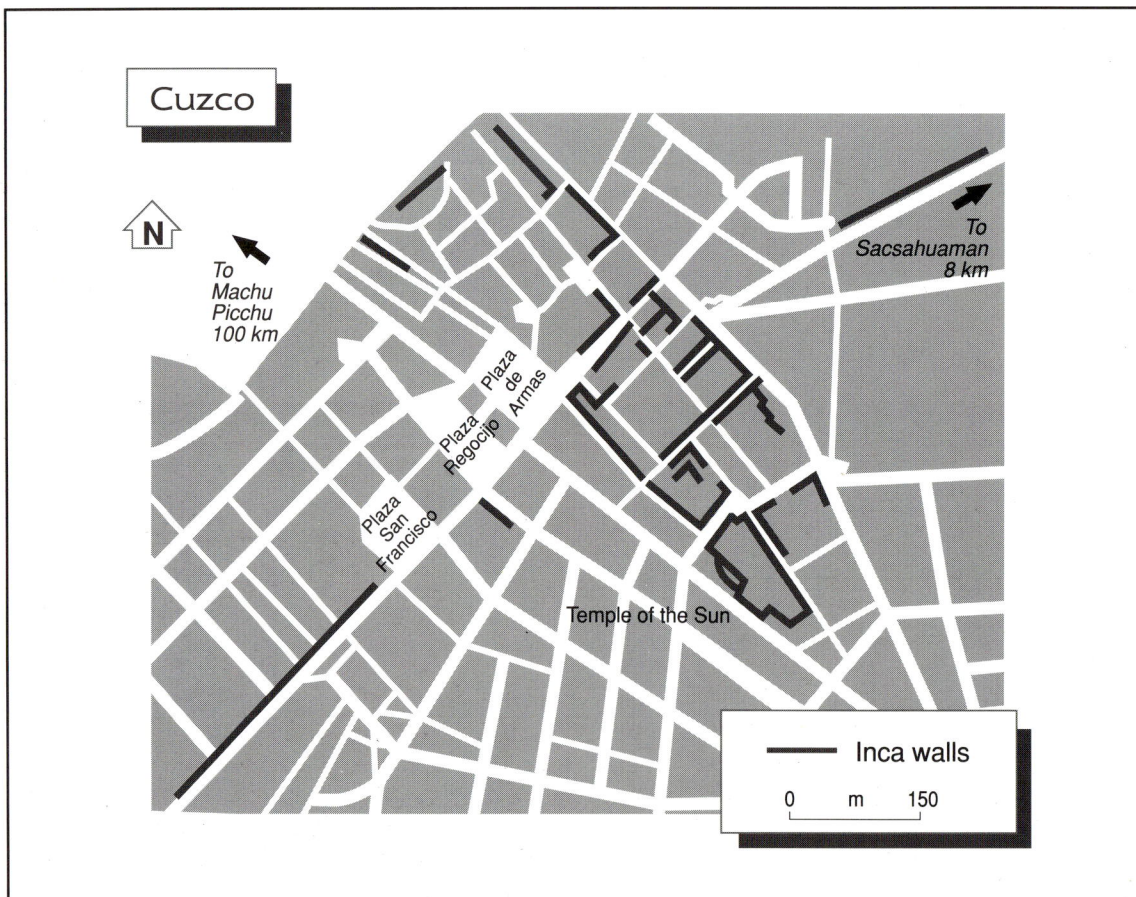

The impressive walls of the fortress of Sacsahuaman, overlooking and protecting the city of Cuzco. The fortress was built with a double wall in a zig-zag shape – some say to imitate the teeth of a jaguar. Thousands of labourers worked for up to 70 years to complete Sacsahuaman. Although its walls are in good condition, there are no buildings standing inside the fortress. Their stones have been removed to help build the modern city of Cuzco.

Cuzco

N

To Machu Picchu 100 km

To Sacsahuaman 8 km

Plaza de Armas

Plaza Regocijo

Plaza San Francisco

Temple of the Sun

Inca walls

0   m   150

population of Cuzco could take shelter inside Sacsahuaman. Aqueducts brought water into the fortress and huge barns full of food meant the inhabitants could withstand a long siege if they were attacked. When the Spaniards came to Cuzco in the 1530s, Sacsahuaman was the scene of many fierce battles. Years later, a Spanish visitor to Cuzco wrote to the king of Spain, 'This is the best and largest city which I have seen...there are buildings which are so beautiful and well built that they would also be remarkable in Spain'.

Fact File

The Inca calendar

The Incas recorded time by calculating the positions of the sun and moon. Outside Cuzco they built four small stone towers. From inside the city the sun could be seen rising above the towers and calculations were made which fixed the time of year. Months were counted from one new moon to the next and an Inca year contained 12 lunar months. From their observations the Incas were able to work out the best times to plant and gather their crops and when certain ceremonies were to be performed. In many Inca towns a special open-air altar was built with an upright stone post in the centre. It acted as a kind of 'sun dial' and the Incas were able to tell the time of day by measuring the length of shadow made by the post. At midday the sun was directly overhead, and no shadow was cast. At Machu Picchu (see page 26) the city's sun clock was built inside the Intihuatana temple, whose name meant the 'place to which the sun is tied'.

The 'sun dial' at Machu Picchu. All major Inca towns had an upright stone such as this, believed to have been for calculating the time and for astronomical observations.

The modern city of Cuzco looking towards the Plaza de Armas square, and the cathedral which is on the left. This square is at the centre of Cuzco, as it was in Inca times. The Incas used the square for their religious festivals and during the days of Spanish control it was the scene of many executions.

Machu Picchu – lost city of the Incas

Machu Picchu is the most famous Inca site in Peru because it has been preserved in such good condition. It lies about 100 kilometres north of Cuzco, the capital. But whereas Cuzco was built in a valley high up on the highland plateau, Machu Picchu was built in the mountains in the lower lying jungle. The city was both a fortress and a refuge for about 1,000 people. It was defended by sheer cliffs which dropped hundreds of metres to the valleys below.

Archaeologists believe that Machu Picchu was built by the Inca emperor Pachacuti, starting in about 1440. It belonged to his royal estate, and was used as a country retreat by nobles and members of the royal family.

Within the city, about 200 stone houses and military buildings were built along terraces. Stairways cut from the rock led from one group of buildings to another and channels flowed with fresh water brought from the snow-covered mountains above the city.

Machu Picchu was occupied by the Incas until the 1570s, and then, incredibly, it was completely forgotten about for over 350 years – not even Francisco Pizarro and his army of Spanish soldiers knew of its existence (see page 41).

In 1911, Hiram Bingham, an archaeologist from Yale University, USA, led an expedition to the area of Machu Picchu

Machu Picchu is often called the 'lost city of the Incas' because it was only rediscovered in the early 1900s.

mountain in search of Inca ruins. After a five-day journey on foot from Cuzco, Bingham's team climbed the overgrown slopes of the mountain. In his notebook he wrote, 'Suddenly we found ourselves in the midst of a jungle-covered maze of small and large walls...surprise followed surprise until there came the realization that we were in the midst of as wonderful ruins as were ever found in Peru'. Bingham returned to Machu Picchu in 1912 and began to excavate the city and learn some of its 'lost' secrets.

Stone walls sloping into the side of a mountain held the terrace soil in place. These are some of the abandoned terraces to be seen at Machu Picchu.

Fact File

Dating Machu Picchu

Hiram Bingham knew that the best way to date the ruins of Machu Picchu was by discovering the graves of the city's inhabitants. The graves would contain certain objects and from these he could work out the age of Machu Picchu by comparing them with objects found at other Inca sites. He found over 100 graves in total, most hidden within small caves on the slopes of the mountains below the city. The dead were buried in sitting positions, with their knees drawn up under their chins. From the painted pottery, bronze tweezers and shawl pins found with the bodies, Bingham was able to tell that Machu Picchu was only occupied in the final years of the Inca empire.

Hiram Bingham called this stone the Funeral Rock. He thought this was where the bodies of dead people from Machu Picchu were brought to dry in the sun, before being taken for burial.

Cluster of houses and other buildings at Machu Picchu.

ORGANIZING THE EMPIRE

Roads and bridges

The Incas were expert road builders. Their vast empire was crossed by a network of around 30,000 kilometres of narrow roads, along which were more than 2,000 way stations where travellers could stop to eat and sleep, and thousands of 'post offices' (see Fact File).

Roads became very important to the Incas as their empire expanded and more and more land came under their control. Good communications were needed in order to keep the empire together. Without a network of roads the Inca empire could have returned to being a group of many small, independent communities – just as it was before the Incas united them.

Inca bridges were considerable feats of civil engineering. Long suspension bridges were made of thick, twisted fibres with thinner fibres woven together for the walkway. Shorter bridges were often made of wood and were more solid than the suspension bridges. A third way of crossing a river or canyon was in a basket which slid along a rope tied between the two sides of the gorge. Bridges were so important that they were inspected by a government official called the 'Guardian of Bridges'. If any faults were found he would order local workers to carry out repairs.

The Incas built two main roads which ran the length of the empire from north to south. Both were given names by the Spaniards. The road along the coast they called the 'Plains Highway' and the one which ran high up in the steep countryside they called the 'Mountain Highway'. Many smaller roads joined the two main roads along their length.

Just as the Romans did in Europe, the Incas believed in building their roads as straight as possible. Where the ground was steep the roads changed to being stairways, winding up and down the hillsides. And where there were rivers or canyons to cross, bridges were built. Because the Incas did not have wheeled vehicles their roads did not have to be very wide. They were built for people on foot and animals only. Inca roads were paved and bumpy ground was levelled with 'pirca' which was a mixture of clay, pebbles and crushed maize leaves.

At frequent intervals there would be a resting place called a 'tambo', where food and shelter could be had for the night – both for the traveller and for the llamas he might have with him.

An Inca road cutting through forest near Machu Picchu.

The Incas built a vast network of roads. Some scaled high mountains, ran through forests and crossed deep gorges. This modern road snakes its way to Machu Picchu.

This military settlement also served as a 'tambo', where travellers could rest and refresh themselves. This example, built of mud-brick, is known as Tambo Colorado and is near the Pacific coast.

Fact File

Taking messages

The Incas had their own postal system. Postmen, called 'chasquis', were trained from childhood to become fast runners. They were highly regarded and carried messages in their heads and statistical information recorded as knots tied in 'quipus' (see page 21). They worked in small groups, running along the roads between 'post offices' where other 'chasquis' were waiting to take over. By using this relay system up to 600 kilometres could be covered in a day. Not only messages were delivered by the Inca postmen. Fresh food such as fish was rushed to Cuzco for the emperor's table – and it had to arrive fresh or there would probably be trouble for the runner!

Doctors and medicine

The Incas thought that all illness entered the body by sorcery. They even thought a person became ill by the wind blowing evil spirits into the body. Because of this, the Incas practised a form of magic which they hoped would make a sick person feel better. If, for example, a person had broken an arm or a leg, they would sacrifice an animal on the exact spot where the accident had happened. By doing this they hoped for a quick recovery and that the gods would protect them from evil.

Inca doctors and healers had a great knowledge of plants, from which they made all kinds of herbal medicines. People who were not fit to do heavy work, such as building roads, helped the doctors in their study of plants. Wounds were healed with the sap of a plant from the pepper family and the leaves of the yuca plant were boiled to make a potion which was good for rheumatism.

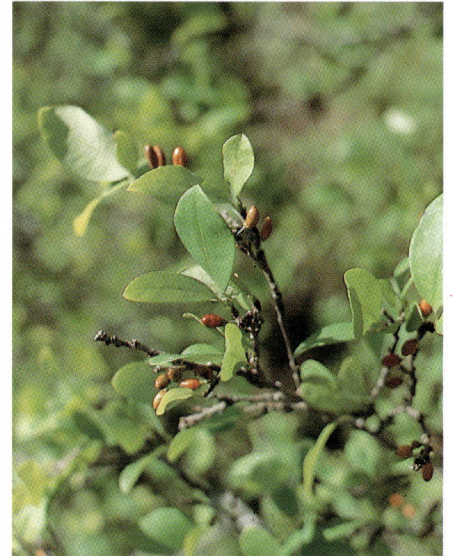

The coca plant which can grow up to two metres tall. Its leaves make the modern drug called cocaine. Coca had great religious significance for the Incas, as it still has today for many people in South America. Its leaves are chewed to release its powerful medicinal properties.

Fact File

Disease

What did the Incas suffer from? The most common illnesses were bronchitis and pneumonia and a type of leprosy called 'uta' was common. Inca surgeons tried to cure it by cutting off the parts of the body which it affected – a drastic measure which was probably worse than the actual disease! When the Spaniards arrived they accidentally brought new diseases with them which infected the Incas. Plague, smallpox, influenza, scarlet fever, measles and chicken pox were unknown to the Incas before the 16th century, and they had no resistance to these new diseases from Europe. Thousands of Incas died as a result of catching these 'foreign' diseases.

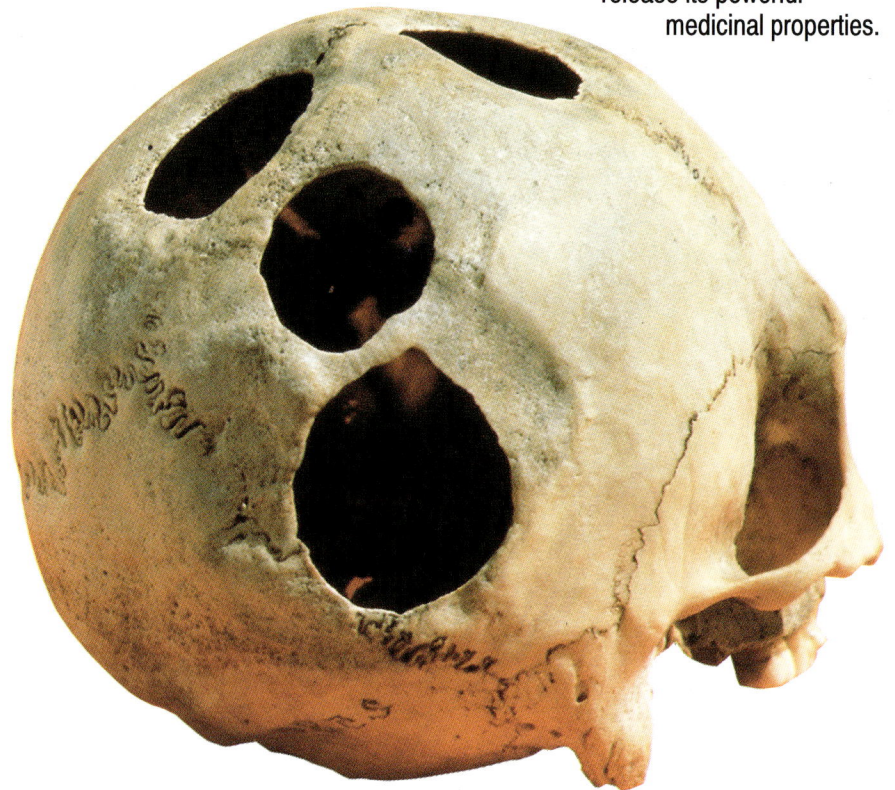

The skull of an Inca which has been 'trepanned'. Note the thin areas of new bone around the holes, showing that this person survived the operations. Inca doctors practised cutting into their patients' skulls to relieve pressures and release evil spirits. One skull has been found where the patient underwent five such operations!

Minerals also had a part to play in Inca medicine. Edible clay was prescribed for gout and crushed jasper was thought to stop bleeding. If evil spirits were present in a house, human excrement was placed inside it: its bad smell was supposed to drive the spirits away – it probably had the same affect on the neighbours! Even urine was considered to be a cure because of the ammonia it contained. It was rubbed on children who had fevers!

Perhaps the most famous Inca medicine was coca, made from the bush of the same name. When its leaves were chewed, a person felt less hunger or tiredness.

Medicines on sale in a street market today. The labels claim that the herbal remedies on this stall are good for diabetes, kidney disorders, for the liver, blisters, stomach and shoulder ache.

This pottery jar of the Moche culture is shaped like the tubers of a yuca plant – important to the Incas both for food and medicine.

The leaves of the yuca plant were used in the treatment of aching joints. This plant, also known as manioc or cassava, is a staple food for many people in South America. Its tubers are eaten boiled or baked and usually served with fish. When dried and ground to a flour it can be made into rounds of unleavened bread.

Inca law

The Incas had a good legal system which helped keep their empire under control. Inca laws were strictly obeyed and throughout the empire civil servants were employed to see that the laws were not broken. There were no prisons but punishments could be very harsh. Ordinary people tended to fear the law, not just obey it.

A person accused of a crime was tried before a court and the trial could last a few days. It was not uncommon for the person to be tortured in order to make him confess to the crime – even though he might have been innocent. Then the judge would pass sentence. Serious crimes resulted in the death sentence, which could be horribly gruesome. Four ways of carrying this out were: beheading, stoning, being thrown off a cliff, or being tossed into a pit full of wild animals or snakes. Less serious crimes could have resulted in a whipping, losing an eye, a hand or foot, losing property or being deported to another part of the empire and never allowed to return home.

The age of a person was taken into account and very young offenders might be given less severe sentences. These were

A small village in modern Peru. Note how the farmland is divided into little enclosed fields – in the days of the Incas each field would have equalled a 'tupu' which was the minimum amount of land needed to support one family. The farmers in this picture are tending to rows of potatoes which have been planted on soil ridges to help water drain away more quickly.

Fact File

Looking after the people

In return for obeying the law, an ordinary Inca was granted certain rights and privileges. He had the right to own an amount of land, called a 'tupu'. On this land an Inca farmer was expected to grow enough food for his family. For each new child in his family he received half a 'tupu' of land more. If a woman's husband died, her land was cultivated for her and in this way neither she nor her family went short of food. In times of famine food was distributed to the needy from the emperor's storehouses.

In Peru there are many steep-sided, rocky gorges. Perhaps this was one of the places from which the Incas hurled criminals to their death.

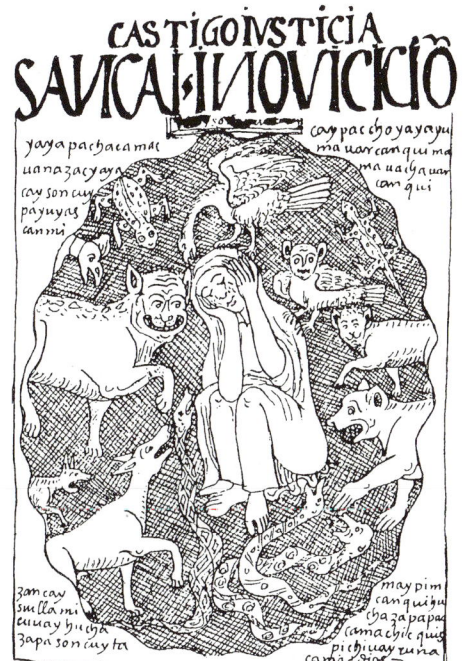

This person has been thrown into a deep pit full of wild animals. In this drawing by Guamán Poma a large bird tugs at the crying man's hair, snakes slither around his feet and dangerous beasts surround him.

intended to act as warnings – next time the sentence might have been tougher. Whether or not the person had been in trouble before was also important.

The overall results of Inca law meant that the empire was well run. People respected the law and knew what to expect should they do wrong. But all this changed with the coming of the Spaniards in the 1500s. Law and order broke down among the Incas. A Spanish missionary saw what had happened and in a letter to the king of Spain he said, 'We have changed the Indians entirely...It seems that at one time evil did not exist, today it is good which seems to have disappeared'.

RELIGIOUS LIFE

Gods, goddesses and priests

As the Incas had no writing of their own, what we know of their religion is based mostly on accounts written by Spanish officials and priests in the 1500s. The problem with this evidence is that it is prejudiced because it uses European ideas to describe an unfamiliar religion.

There were many gods and goddesses in the Inca religion. Each was said to have magical powers and was responsible for looking after a different part of Inca life. As most Incas led lives connected with the land they believed their gods had the power to look after their farms, crops and animals. Offerings were made to all the gods – the poorest people would offer some of their eyelashes!

One important god was Viracocha while two others were Inti, the sun god, and Quilla, the moon god. Some Inca temples were so closely connected with the worship of the sun that the Spaniards called them 'sun temples'. Inside the temples were discs of beaten gold, each one representing

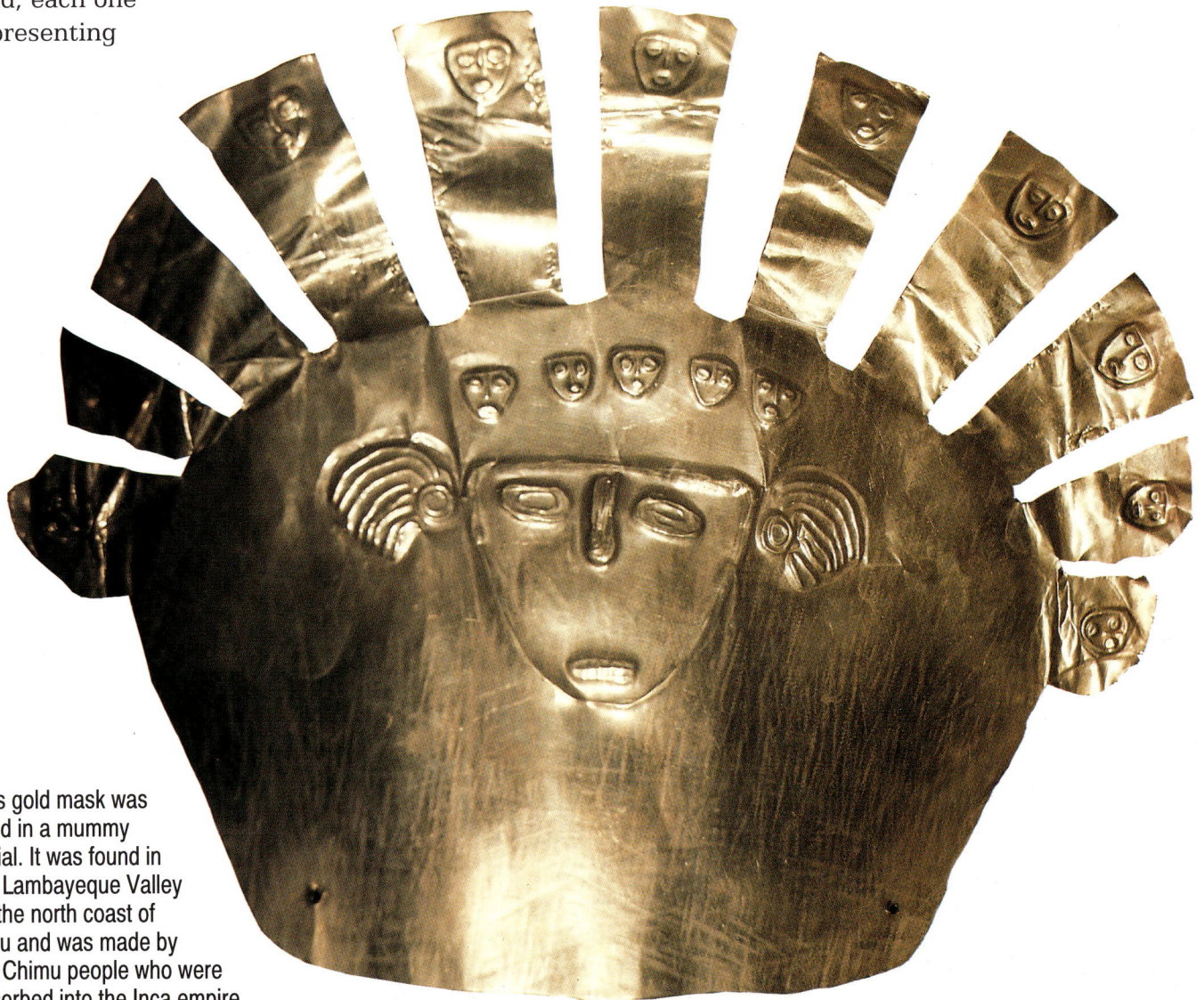

This gold mask was used in a mummy burial. It was found in the Lambayeque Valley on the north coast of Peru and was made by the Chimu people who were absorbed into the Inca empire.

the sun and all its power. The father and mother of the sun and moon was the one god Viracocha. He reigned supreme and was often depicted as an old man with white hair and a beard.

Inca temples could be small, single-roomed buildings in remote valleys, or large, sprawling complexes housing many priests and their attendants. The main temple was at Cuzco, the Inca capital, and this was where the high priest lived. He was a relative of the emperor. Other people who lived in the temples were lesser priests, monks and servants. Priests were called upon to make sacrifices to the gods (see page 36), cure illnesses, foretell the future and generally care for the lives of the people in their area.

INCA RELIGIOUS ORDER

High priest	Head of all priests in the Inca empire. He lived in Cuzco and was usually a brother of the Inca emperor.
High priestess	The daughter of a leading noble. Together with the wife of the Inca emperor she led many important religious festivals.
Priests	Lived in temples throughout the empire, and served the needs of the local communities. They also used magic and could talk to spirits.
Mamacunas	Teacher-nuns who educated girls who would grow up to become sun virgins.
Sun virgins or Acllas	Daughters of nobles who spent their lives serving at temples. Some became Mamacunas and passed their knowledge on to the next generation of sun virgins.
Healers	People who practised herbal medicine.

Some people who live in Peru today still hold on to part of the ancient Inca religion. They still leave offerings at places they believe are special for them, as at this 'huaca' or sacred place. Around the Inca capital of Cuzco were more than 300 'huacas', many of them tombs containing the mummies of Inca nobles. They were all thought to be connected by imaginary lines.

Fact File

Sacred places

One of the most important aspects of Inca religion was the 'huaca'. This was any place or object that held a religious meaning and could therefore be regarded as sacred. Whenever an Inca approached a 'huaca' he did so with care, in case he annoyed the spirit or god. The Inca would leave an offering, perhaps food or clothing, and this would stop the spirit from doing any damage. All kinds of places or objects could become 'huacas', from great hills to strangely-shaped rocks and springs along a road. The Incas believed that spirits had both good and evil characters. There were no spirits or gods who were purely good or evil.

SIX INCA GODS

Viracocha	*An ancestor and weather god who was both the father and the mother of Inti and Quilla.*
Inti	*The sun god whose warmth caused the crops to grow.*
Illapa	*A god of thunder and lightning.*
Pachamama	*The earth goddess in whose soil the crops grew.*
Mamacocha	*The sea goddess who gave the Incas their fish.*
Quilla	*The moon god.*

Sacrifices and festivals

To the Incas, sacrifices were not acts of cruelty but an essential way of life designed to please the gods.

All kinds of sacrifices were made. The simplest sacrifices were offerings of food and drink left at 'huacas' – places or objects that were considered spirits or gods (see page 35). If the worshipper had no food to leave as he passed an 'huaca', then he might leave a few plucked hairs or eyebrows as an offering. Wealthier

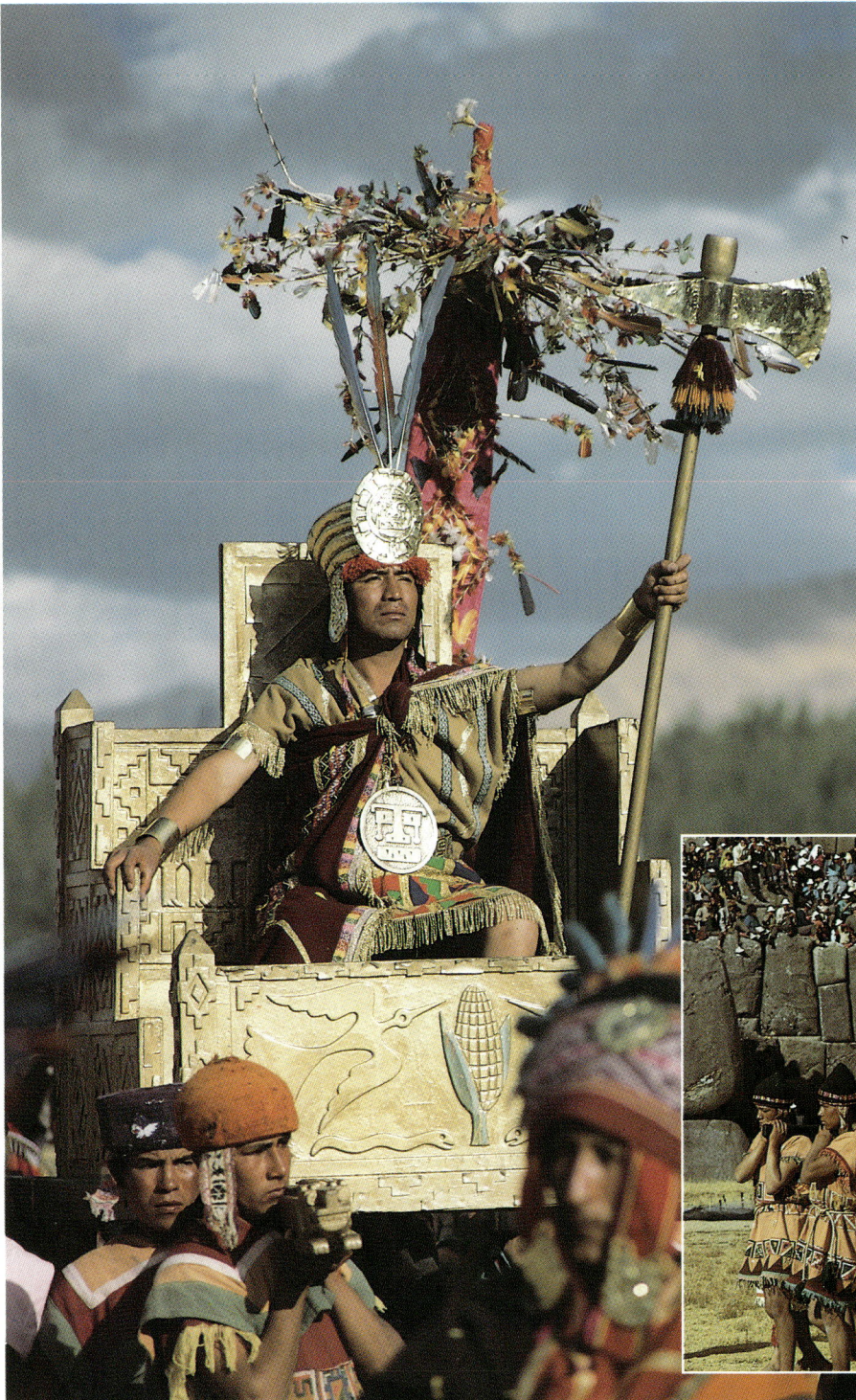

There were many important festivals in the Inca year. Some marked the stages in a person's life and others were connected with agriculture. The Capac Raymi festival celebrated the coming of age for young nobles where the men underwent ritual battles and a death-defying foot race. Another festival was Sitwa, in early September, when all foreigners had to leave Cuzco for a time. One festival is still performed today – for the benefit of tourists. This is the festival of Inti Raymi (the Festival of the Sun). It is held at the mid-winter solstice on 24 June to welcome the return of the sun. The festival is within the walls of the fortress of Sacsahuaman, at Cuzco, and features an Inca emperor, nobles and many dancers.

people might leave a piece of expensive cloth or a small gold charm. The preserved bodies of emperors also received regular offerings.

Sacrifices of living animals were common. Llamas, alpacas and guinea-pigs were offered to the gods in public ceremonies which attracted many people. Brown llamas were sacrificed to Viracocha, the ancestor and weather god, white llamas to Inti, the sun god, and mottled llamas to Illapa, the weather god.

Human sacrifices, usually of children, were also a part of Inca religion. They were important sacrifices and were offered to the gods only in times of great turmoil, at the coronation of a new emperor or in time of famine. The children, both boys and girls, were aged about ten years old. They were fit and strong and were given a special meal before being killed. In some cases families offered their children to be sacrificed, but in others the priests chose those they wanted.

This man is holding a headdress made of gold. It was found by archaeologists at Sipán, in the tomb of a Moche king. He would have worn the headdress on special occasions.

Fact File

Inca festivals

The Inca year was full of festivals. Almost every day there was something to be celebrated and in most cases the festivals were linked to events in the farming year. Planting seeds and harvesting crops were both times of great agricultural importance. At these times the temple priests would lead processions and offer sacrifices. Sacred objects, including the preserved bodies of dead emperors, were brought from the temples and carried through the streets of Cuzco. The sight of such important relics reassured the gathered crowds that all was well and that the gods were being properly looked after.

During the course of some festivals in Cuzco the preserved bodies of long dead emperors and their queens were carried through the streets from morning until night, as shown in this drawing by Guamán Poma. The mummies were carried from one tomb to another, making 'visits' to each other and having 'conversations'. Finally they were all brought into the main square in the city where they sat in state before being taken back to their tombs.

Death and burial

The Incas believed in life after death. But not only that, they practised the worship of their dead ancestors and emperors.

When an Inca died, his body was treated in a special way. His internal organs were removed, his legs pulled up and his knees tucked under his chin. The dead Inca was then wrapped in layers of cloth, placed inside a large cotton bag and tightly bound with ropes. A procession carried the body to a small cave or to a specially prepared stone tomb, shaped like a small tower or bee-hive. Offerings of food and the belongings of the dead person were left in the tomb. In the dry atmosphere of the Andes the body soon dried out and reached the point at which it stopped decaying. An Inca cemetery was usually in a place unsuitable for farming.

When an Inca emperor died his dried body was waited on as if it was still alive, even to the point of having attendants stand nearby to fan flies away! On the death of the emperor, some of his favourite wives and servants might be executed in order to travel with him into the next world where they could continue to serve him. Each year the dried bodies of the Inca emperors were displayed at public ceremonies in Cuzco. The last time this happened was in 1559.

The Spaniards had never seen preserved bodies before and between 1615 and 1619 they collected 1,365 dried bodies of dead Incas as macabre souvenirs, and many were destroyed as objects of idol worship.

A preserved body tightly wrapped in ropes.

A burial tower at Sillustani belonging to a group of people conquered by the Incas. This one was built about AD 1000. The tower was a tomb for one or more bodies. Some towers were probably family vaults used over many generations of the same family.

Fact File

Life after death

The Incas believed in a life after death. They believed that the spirits of dead people travelled to be with the sun god, Inti, but only if those people had been good during their time on Earth. In this warm, friendly other world, the lucky people never wanted – there was always food to eat and they were guaranteed a good and happy life. But if they had sinned in any way during their time on Earth, then their punishment was a life after death in the dark, unfriendly underworld where it was always cold and they would have only rocks for food. No wonder the Incas cared so much about saying their prayers and leaving offerings at their many sacred places!

An Inca mummy bundle. Inside the bundle is the dead person, wrapped in ropes. A clay mask covers his face and he is dressed in his everyday clothes.

A cemetery at Nazca in the south of Peru. The sand and the dryness of the local desert protected finely woven textiles in which the bodies had been wrapped. The cemetery belonged to people of the Nazca culture who lived 500 – 1,000 years before the Incas – but it is interesting to note that both the Nazca people and the Incas practised a similar form of burial technique. Some of the people buried here had had their skulls trepanned (see page 30), where metal plates had been inserted to replace pieces of skull broken by stones hurled from slings.

END OF THE INCA EMPIRE

Arrival of the Spaniards

Christopher Columbus sailed to America in 1492, and on his return to Europe news of the 'New World' he had found spread quickly. Other explorers and fortune hunters followed and made contact with the native Americans, such as the Aztecs of Mexico and the Incas of Peru. Soon, Europe was full of rumours about fabulous treasure in these new and distant lands, and gold-hungry people made plans to capture it for themselves.

The empire of the Aztecs (in Mexico) was defeated by a Spanish army in 1521 – its treasure plundered and its population attacked

This map shows how much land the Spanish governed in North and South America by the year 1600, a little more than 100 years after Columbus had discovered the 'New World'.

Spanish Empire in the Americas

San Juan (1598)
Monterrey (1600)
Guadalajara (1551)
St Augustine (1565)
Havana (1515)
Cuba
Hispaniola
ATLANTIC OCEAN
Guatemala (1542)
Caracas (1567)
Panama (1519)
Santa Fé de Bogota (1538)
Equator
Quito (1534)
Lima (1536)
PACIFIC OCEAN
La Plata (1538)
Asunción (1537)
Santiago (1544)
Buenos Aires (1536)

0   km   1500

■ Spanish Empire in the Americas in about 1600

• Spanish settlement with date of foundation

A ceremonial axe made of gold by the Moche people of Peru. The Spaniards came to Peru in search of valuable objects like this.

by smallpox, a disease unknown in the Americas until it was taken there by Europeans.

In 1532 the Spanish turned their attention towards Peru, where they believed more treasure was to be found. Under the Spanish commander, Francisco Pizarro, a small army of only 180 soldiers landed at the northern town of Tumbes. The bearded, white-skinned men from Spain were the first Europeans the Incas had ever seen, and they were amazed. At first the Incas thought the Spaniards were their own gods who had come to visit them. They thought that Pizarro was Viracocha, one of their most important gods (see page 34). How wrong they were!

Pizarro's small army, with horses, guns, cannons and armour, far outmatched the Incas. Pizarro entered a vulnerable country, made weak by civil war (see page 42) and ravaged by a plague which the Spaniards had accidentally introduced into Mexico 40 years earlier, and which had spread south to Peru.

The end of the Inca empire came suddenly and dramatically. It collapsed within just 30 years of the arrival of the Spaniards.

Gold figures such as those on these pages caused the Spaniards to believe in the story of 'El Dorado' – 'The Gilded Man'.

Fact File

'El Dorado'

Francisco Pizarro was one of the many Spanish 'conquistadores' (conquerors) who sailed to South America in search of new lands and treasure in the 1500s. Like many other Europeans, Pizarro had heard tales about the 'golden kingdoms' of South America and he went to Peru in search of the legendary kingdom which the Spaniards called 'El Dorado'. Translated into English, 'El Dorado' meant 'The Gilded Man' (gilding means 'covered with gold'). Stories reached Europe in the 1500s about a chieftain from a tribe in South America who was so wealthy that he could afford to cover himself from head to toe in gold dust, before washing it off in a sacred lake. Pizarro knew this story, but, whatever the truth about 'El Dorado', he never found it. Nor did anyone else, but even today there are adventurers convinced that it exists somewhere.

Francisco Pizarro (1478–1541), the leader of a small Spanish army that conquered the Inca empire in the 1530s.

A drawing by Guamán Poma that compares the arms and armour of a Spanish foot soldier with those of an Inca. The Spaniard wears steel armour from head to toe and carries a steel shield and a weapon probably made of iron. He may also have had a firearm such as a musket. The Inca soldier wears cotton clothing and carries a wooden shield. His weapons are a spear with a copper or stone tip and a mace with a stone head.

Atahuallpa – the last Inca emperor

Atahuallpa became emperor when he defeated his half-brother, Huascar, in a civil war following the death of their father, the emperor Huayna Capc. Atahuallpa's troops captured Huascar and executed him – so much for brotherly love! These events happened in 1532 – the same year that Francisco Pizarro and his Spanish army landed at Tumbes in the north of Peru, about 1,600 kilometres from Cuzco.

Pizarro and Atahuallpa met at the Inca town of Cajamarca on 16 November 1532. Pizarro had an army of 180 men and Atahuallpa was supported by thousands of Inca soldiers. According to Spanish accounts, at their meeting a Dominican monk handed Atahuallpa a bible. He examined it but as it meant nothing to him he threw it to the ground. The Spanish soldiers rushed forward, firing their guns at the Incas. Atahuallpa was taken prisoner and as many as 6,000 of his soldiers were killed.

Atahuallpa learned of the Spaniards' interest in gold and he offered to fill a large room with precious objects in return for his freedom. Gold was brought by llama trains and carriers from all parts of the empire and soon the room was full. But Pizarro charged Atahuallpa with killing Huascar and planning an uprising against the Spaniards. He was found guilty and sentenced to death by burning. Then, at the last moment he was told the sentence would be changed to death by garrotte if he accepted Christianity. He did, and on 29 August 1533 the last Inca emperor was baptized, tied to a stake and executed in the public square of Cajamarca.

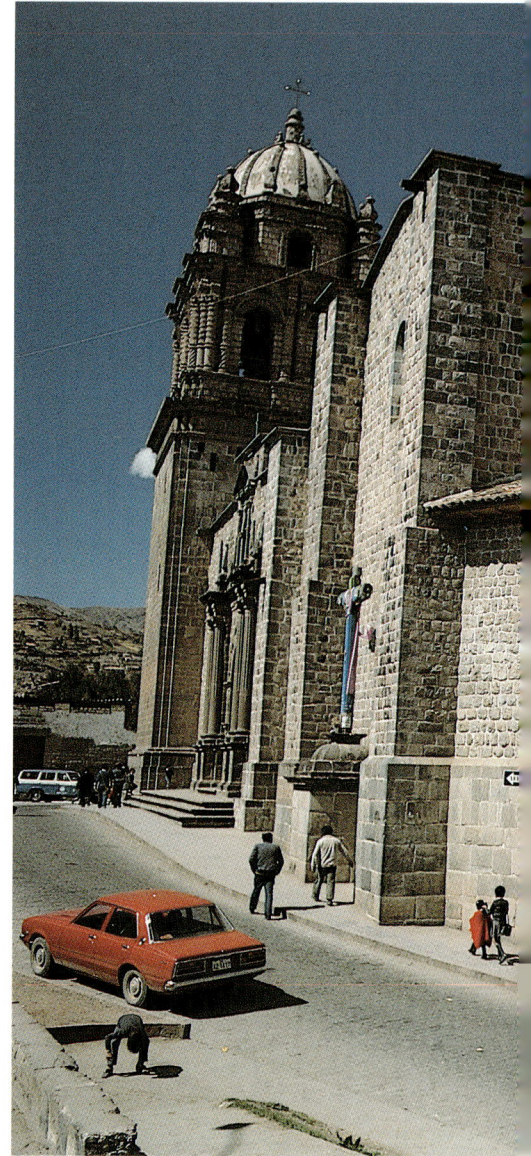

The fatal moment at Cajamarca as a bible is thrown to the ground.

A drawing by Guamán Poma showing Atahuallpa in prison with a guard. Note how his hands and legs are bound.

A Christian monastery, St Domingo, built over the Inca sun temple of Koricancha, Cuzco.

The Spaniards built this church in the Urubamba Valley from where missionaries were sent out in an attempt to convert the Incas to Christianity.

Fact File

Missionaries

It was not only Spanish soldiers who went to Peru. The Catholic church in both Spain and Portugal, on hearing of the discovery of the New World, sent missionaries. Their task was to convert the Incas and the other communities of South America to Christianity. The missionaries built churches and mission houses. Gradually they succeeded in turning the Incas away from their own gods, such as Viracocha, persuading them to believe in the bible and the Christian church. While the soldiers conquered the empire of the Incas, the European missionaries conquered their souls. But it must be said that many of the native peoples only accepted Christianity as a way to conceal their deeper belief in their ancient gods.

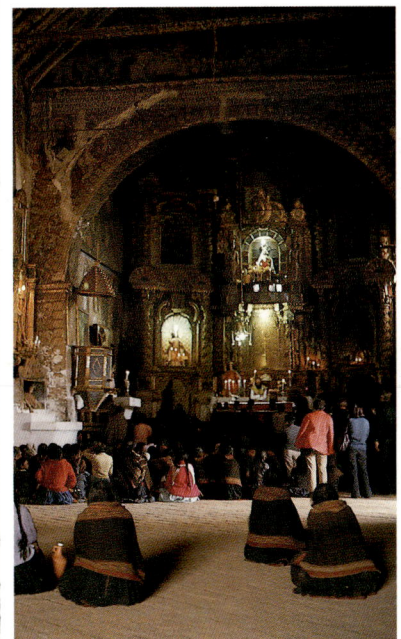
Peruvians at Mass in a church near Cuzco.

43

Discovering the Incas

Archaeologists have been curious about the Incas for a long time, but it is really only since Hiram Bingham's work at Machu Picchu (see page 26) that evidence of their great empire has really come to light. Of course, people had known about the wealth of the Inca empire since the Spaniards began to take Inca gold back to Europe in the 1500s. But apart from that, little was known of their actual culture – how they lived. Bingham knew that there was more to the Incas than just objects made from gold, and he set out to discover their 'lost' world.

Today's archaeologists have many ways of working. They may find out about new sites from rumours amongst local people that tell of treasure being found, as at Sipán (see page 10). Or they may systematically survey an area from the air, flying over it in a small aeroplane taking photographs which can be studied carefully later.

When a site is excavated, the archaeologists may sieve the soil, looking for minute objects which would otherwise be missed. In this way such things as fish bones and tiny beads may be found, telling the experts what the Incas ate and wore.

Archaeologists at Sipán, carefully removing layers of soil.

An archaeologist at work on a modern excavation in Peru. He is making a detailed drawing of the 'Lord of Sipán' (see page 10).

A busy street in Lima, the modern capital of Peru and where over 8 million of the country's 26 million people live.

In their laboratories, the archaeologists piece together broken pots, make drawings and take photographs. All the objects they find on their excavations will go to a museum, and some of them will go on display for the public to see. The story of the Incas will be told to thousands of people who will never go on an excavation themselves, or actually go to Peru – the land of the Incas.

Incas today

Are there any Incas alive today? The answer is 'yes', because some Peruvians can trace their family trees right back to the time of the Incas, 500 years ago. And in towns and villages throughout Peru, people still use llamas, make similar sorts of pottery, wear similar clothes and weave similar patterns just as their Inca ancestors did. But the presence of Spain is felt strongly, both in the language spoken in Peru today and in the Christian religion practised there.

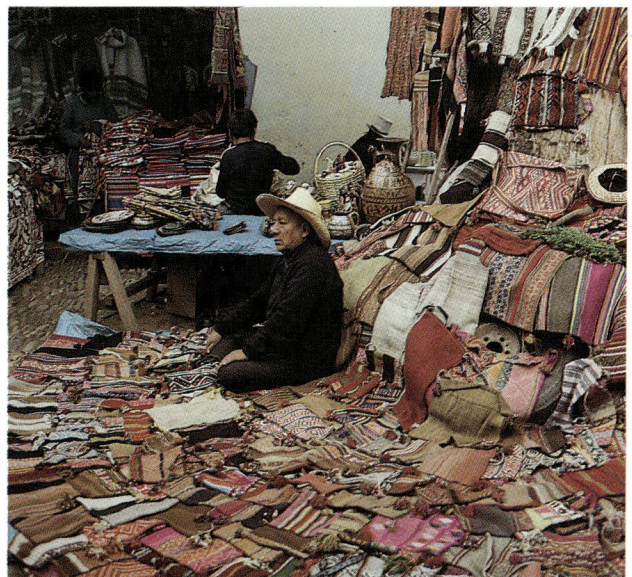

A present day market in Peru. Notice the colours and patterns of the cloth for sale on this stall.

GLOSSARY

Alpaca – A small mountain animal raised by the Incas for its fine wool.

Andes – A mountain chain that stretches the length of South America for 6,500 kilometres.

Atahuallpa – Last Inca emperor, executed by the Spaniards. Reigned 1532–1533.

Hiram Bingham (1875–1919) – Archaeologist who discovered Machu Picchu in 1911.

Cajamarca – Town in the north of Peru where Atahuallpa was executed.

Chasqui – Runner who carried messages along the Inca road system.

Christopher Columbus (1451–1506) – Italian explorer who, in 1492, 'discovered' the Americas.

Coca – A shrub from which the drug cocaine is obtained.

Conquistador – A member of the first group of Spanish conquerors who took part in the conquest of Central and South America.

Coya – An Inca queen who was the emperor's chief wife and his own sister.

Cuzco – Capital city of the Incas.

El Dorado – The Spanish name for a land of gold.

Garrotte – Method of strangulation favoured by the Spaniards.

Guano – Bird droppings used as fertilizer.

Huascar – Inca emperor and half-brother of Atahuallpa. Reigned 1525–1532.

Huaca – A sacred place or object where prayers were said and offerings were left to the gods.

Huaca del Sol – Massive mud-brick pyramid built by the Moche people.

Inca – At first, only the members of a few related families from Cuzco were Incas, but later the name was used for all the people who came under Inca rule.

Llama – Mountain animal, larger than an alpaca, raised by the Incas for its wool and used to carry loads and also in religious ceremonies.

Lima – Modern capital of Peru, founded by the conquistador Francisco Pizarro in 1535.

Machu Picchu – The so-called 'lost city of the Incas' found by Hiram Bingham in 1911.

Mama Huaco – Sister of Manco Capac, who with her brother, founded Cuzco.

Manco Capac – The legendary founder of the Inca people and said to be the first emperor.

Mitima – Process of moving a defeated tribe away from its homeland and settling its people elsewhere in the Inca empire.

Moche – A group of people that lived in north Peru several centuries before the Incas.

Mud-brick – Small bricks made from mud that set hard in the sun. Also called adobe bricks.

Mummy – Any well-preserved body.

New World – The lands of North, South and Central America, 'new' to the European explorers of the 15th and 16th centuries.

Pachacuti – Inca emperor who began to create the empire of the Incas. Reigned 1438–1471.

Philip III (1578–1621) – King of Spain to whom Guamán Poma wrote. Reigned 1598–1621

Pirca – Mixture of clay, pebbles and maize leaves used to level bumpy roads.

Francisco Pizarro (1478–1541) – Spanish leader who conquered the Inca empire in the 1530s.

Platform – A type of raised mud-brick building.

Guamán Poma (c.1525–c.1620) – Chieftain from a tribe conquered by the Incas. He sent an illustrated letter to King Philip III of Spain, describing the life of the Incas.

Pre-Columbian – The time before the arrival of Columbus and other Europeans in the Americas.

Pyramid – A tall flat-topped mound made of mud-brick.

Quechua – The language of the Incas, still spoken today.

Quipu – A counting device made from knotted string.

Sacsahuaman – Massive stone fortress built to defend Cuzco.

Sapa Inca – The official title of the Inca emperor which meant the 'only' Inca.

Sipán – Settlement of the Moche people at which a wealthy burial has been found.

Taclla – A wooden digging stick.

Tambo – A resting place for travellers.

Terraces – Steps cut into the sides of hills and planted with crops.

Titicaca – The world's highest navigable lake.

Trepan – A medical technique used to bore holes into a person's skull. Thought to relieve pressure and release demons.

Tupu – The piece of land owned by an Inca.

Vicuña – A smaller relative of the llama prized by the Incas for its fine wool.

INDEX

Page numbers in **bold** refer to illustrations or their captions.

FURTHER READING

If you want to find out more about the Incas, these books will help:

Aztec, Inca, and Maya, Elizabeth Baquedano (Dorling Kindersley, Eyewitness Books, 2005)
The Ancient Inca, Patricia Calvert (Franklin Watts, 2005)
Find Out About The Incas, Philip Steele (Southwater, 2003)
Ancient America: Cultural Atlas for Young People, Marion Wood (Facts on File, 1990)